IN A DAZE WORK

A PICK-YOUR-
PATH JOURNEY
THROUGH THE
DAILY GRIND

SIOBHÁN GALLAGHER

A TarcherPerigee Book

An imprint of Penguin Random House LLC
375 Hudson Street
New York, New York 10014

TarcherPerigee with tp colophon is a registered trademark
of Penguin Random House LLC.

Most TarcherPerigee books are available at special quantity discounts for bulk
purchase for sales promotions, premiums, fund-raising, and educational needs.
Special books or book excerpts also can be created to fit specific needs. For
details, write: SpecialMarkets@penguinrandomhouse.com.

ISBN 9780143130284

Printed in the United States of America
1   3   5   7   9   10   8   6   4   2

BOOK DESIGN BY SIOBHÁN GALLAGHER

For Mom, Dad, Sean, and Seamus.

I'm so lucky to be a part of this weirdo family.

You are here.

Well, here more specifically.

It is the brief moment between sleep and consciousness.

You're unsure what day it is and exactly who you are.

You're blissfully unaware of all the day's obligations and concerns.

You're hardly even You yet. . . .

Aaaand the moment's over. You blink awake. What day is it?

If it's the weekend, go to page **81**.

If it's a weekday, go to **the next page**.

Your alarm goes off. Do you hit the snooze button?

If you get up, go to **the next page**.

If you hit the snooze button, go to page **26**.

LET'S GET READY TO GRRUUUM MMBLLE!

Okay. Time to get up.

But first: Is it too early to creep your ex?

If you think, "Nah, creep away," go to **the next page**.

If you believe that you should have more self-control, go to page **15**.

Before you even type the first letter of your ex's name into the search bar, you see you received a number of messages from your old friend Jenna, who only talks to you when in need of relationship advice. By the time you respond, her dilemma has been solved. Time for a shower.

You bought your shampoo and conditioner at the same time but the conditioner always seems to run out first.

On your way out the door you spot a spindly, scary bug and immediately step into action. It's dead under your foot within seconds so, okay, it's not even 9:00 AM and you've already killed something today. You can deal with that.

8 : 28 AM

You are held up by someone who obviously doesn't know
how to use a public transit turnstile. Ugh!
You watch your train come and go.

Luckily you spot the redheaded man with the stroller ahead of you who is your daily indicator that you're running on time.

Eventually you squeeze onto the next crowded train and stand in front of a mother and three daughters, each identical and smaller than the last, like a family of nesting dolls.

DIAGRAM OF AWKWARD
ELEVATOR BEHAVIOR

Cleaning your computer desktop makes you feel productive

without actually doing much.

Go to page **35**.

7:48 AM

You have a shower and wipe the steamy condensation from your mirror afterward. You face yourself and correct your posture.

15

7: 52 AM

BEFORE   AFTER

You should have left that pimple alone.

OUT-THE-DOOR CHECKLIST

☑ PHONE
☑ CARDS
☑ LIPSTICK
☑ POCKET
   TRASH

☑ KEYS
☑ EMERGENCY
   PACK OF
   CIGARETTES
   IN CASE YOU
   GET STRESSED

AAAND ☑ UNEASY SENSE OF DOOM!

Good to go!

You leave for work on time. Look at you! Good job.

COMMUTER

You find a seat on the train among your fellow commuters.
There is a mutual understanding among this crowd
of the golden rules of subway etiquette.

COMMUNITY

You must: Be careful about lingering eye contact, smile at babies with exhausted parents, and always double-check if big tote bags are carrying scared tiny dogs. It's the morning and people are tired, so basically, don't be a jerk.

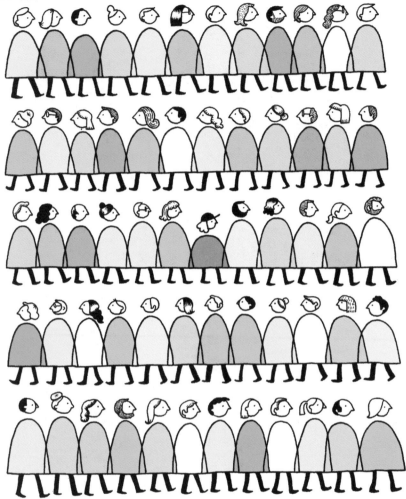

You're in everyone's way and everyone is in yours.

Emerging from the subway station, you walk up the steps two at a time

(the sound of someone's clicking heels behind you

makes you feel rushed and anxious).

You arrive at work. You debate detouring past Deb's desk to see if she brought in any baked goods, and, in the end, your sweet tooth wins.

So that's a no on homemade cookies then.

Go to page **33**.

Big mistake. You sleep in.

You rinse your pits over the bathroom sink and race out the door to catch a bus. Aaaand of course it hits every red light. Ugh, just look at those moseying pedestrians, not a care in the world, no concern if they're holding up traffic. Everyone is already the worst today!

WHAT'S YOUR EXCUSE?

A) THE TRAIN WAS DOWN!

B) AN EMERGENCY WITH YOUR ROOMMATE!

C) YOU FOUND A WOUNDED DOG AND CALLED ANIMAL CONTROL!

D) THERE WAS A FIRE/FLOOD/BREAK-IN AT YOUR BUILDING!

(IT DOESN'T REALLY MATTER—SHE'LL BE ANNOYED EITHER WAY.)

You start racking your brain for potential excuses to tell your boss why you're late. If it sounds like a genuine emergency, maybe she'll be sympathetic! Start practicing your apologetic facial expression.

9:44 AM

You finally arrive at the office. A plane flies overhead
and you can't see what its banner is advertising but you can imagine.

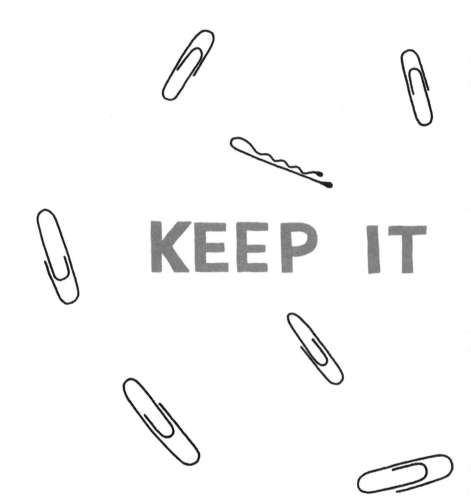

It turns out a few other people are running late this morning too.

TOGETHER

Your boss is out. All is well.

You can finally go to the bathroom. While in the stall, someone else walks in. You shuffle your feet so they know they're not alone and focus your attention on the floor tile that resembles a bear.

You hear a coworker crack his knuckles at the next desk.

Does this make you want to do the same?

If yes, go to **the next page**.

If no, go to page **35**.

That was satisfying.

☑ MAKE TO-DO LIST _____

☑ CHECK EMAIL _____

💀 _____

💀 _____

💀 _____

💀 _____

You check off and accomplish as many menial tasks as possible but a number of deadlines still loom over your to-do list.

* CALL MOM

GEOGRAPHICALLY

GARLIC	GRAPHIC
HIP	PLAY
HOP	PAY
GRAPH	PRAY
PORE	HALL
HARP	LAY
PHALLIC	AGILE
PAGE	CORE
GAG	GORE
PAGE	GORILLA
ROYAL	RAY
YOGA	HAY
RAGE	CHEAP
CALL	HEAP
CLAY	CHILL
GARAGE	LARGE
GIRL	

You bring your notepad to a budget meeting but end up using it to find all the words that can be found in the word "geographically." After the meeting a coworker invites you to join a group going out for lunch. Do you join?

If you join them for lunch, go to page **38**.

If you would rather be alone, go to **the next page**.

You walk to the nearby park and take a seat. You watch the man across from you carefully peel the saran wrap from his sandwich. You think of him preparing this little meal for himself this morning, maybe the same way his mother used to, with an extra mayo smiley face before closing it.

Go to page **43**.

Lots of options at the restaurant.

You want to pick wisely.

You finally place your order. The server's name is Judy, and you initially feel close to her since she shares the same name as a friend from back home, but you quickly realize that's where their similarities end. *Your* Judy is funny and always excited to see you. But this one isn't nice to you at all! Your Judy is so much better.

You settled for an elaborate pasta dish, but when you see
your friend's chicken sandwich arrive at the table,
you know you made the wrong choice.

INDISTINGUISHABLE
STAIN

SUSPICIOUS SMEAR,
HEH HEH HEH

After the meal, you find the dirtiest-looking bill in your wallet
to leave for Judy. You're still going to tip her,
but certainly not with a fresh, clean bill.
That'll show her!

Later, back in the office, you decide it's finally time to make

the simple phone call you've been putting off.

Or maybe it can wait until tomorrow. . . .

Uh-oh, you cause a paper jam in the printer. But no worries, you have a tried-and-true six-step method and know just what to do.

At last, it's quitting time.

Now for tonight: You had tentative plans to get drinks with some guy named Tyler, but your friend Wes also invited you to join him and friends for happy hour.

If you want to go on the date, go to **the next page**.

To meet your friend Wes, go to page **68**.

To skip the whole "socializing" thing and just head home, go to page **58**.

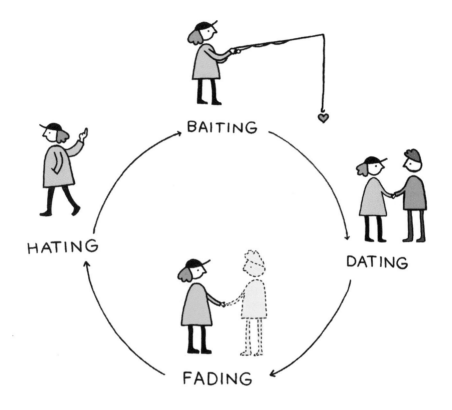

BAITING

DATING

FADING

HATING

Alright, guess you can go through this ritual once again.

5 O'CLOCK SHADOW

You make your way toward the bar
through the crowd of fellow 9-to-5ers.

Dates make you nervous. You arrive a good 50 minutes early and decide to

kill time at your favorite nearby bookstore.

Unfortunately, once the date begins,
you wish you'd stayed at the bookstore.

In the middle of the third story about his facial hair, Tyler confirms your
suspicion that he's the kind of guy who is so lacking in personality that he
grew a beard just so he'd have something to talk about. You shift your
attention to the fish tank near your table and find yourself feeling
jealous of the small scuba diving figure.

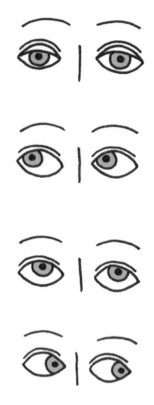

Fig. 1: THE PERFECT EYE ROLL

You say your goodbyes with Tyler and head to the nearest bus home. On the bright side, you're pretty sure you perfected the eye roll tonight.

Go to page **54**.

You lazily scroll through friends' posts online, reflecting on the state of the world. Suddenly, your laptop crashes and you're left looking at your own reflection (at a very unflattering angle). This is your cue to close your device.

Go to page **78**.

WHO NEEDS EYE CONTACT ANYWAY?

LONG-TERM PARTNERS, RECENTLY MARRIED

You pass a restaurant brightly showcasing a variety of date nights

PATIENT, SLEEPY, HAPPY

FIRST DATE. THEY WON'T LAST.
POOR GIRL, YOU CAN CERTAINLY RELATE.

You guess the stories of each couple as you pass their window.

While waiting for the bus, you see a group approaching.

You mute your music and keep an eye on them as they pass.

The bus soon arrives to take you home. You smile at a kid seated
in front of you who gets scolded by his mother for writing in the
condensation on the window. You think it's funny and are impressed
he can spell so well backward.

Go to page 77.

On the way home you pick up some toilet paper and spot some granola bars that are on a sale so good, it'd be dumb not to buy them! The packaging makes them look healthy, so you don't bother checking the nutrition facts. You wait in line and scan the magazines on display. Sad selection.

On the train, you sit across from a little boy rubbing his mother's arm, and you're immediately endeared. However, you soon notice that he's not lovingly stroking her sleeve, but rather wiping his cheese-dusted fingers on her shirt.

Once you get off the train and make your way home, you notice
some guy yelling at you. You try to ignore him and when he realizes he's not
getting any kind of response from you, he calls you a witch.
How did he know?! You hop on your broomstick and fly home.

You arrive. Are your roommates home?

If they are, go to page **63**.

If no one else is home, go to **the next page**.

Well, in that case . . .

B I N G O
WITH MOM

SHE ASKS WHAT MEALS YOU MAKE FOR YOURSELF	SHE WANTS REASSURANCE YOUR HEALTH IS A-OK	SHE ASKS IF SHE CAN FINALLY TOSS OUT YOUR BOX OF TEEN MAGAZINES FROM THE '90S IN THE BASEMENT	SHE TELLS YOU ABOUT ALL HER FRIEND'S KIDS GETTING MARRIED AND HAVING KIDS	YOU BOTH PROVIDE WEATHER UPDATES
SHE ASKS IF YOU WANT HER TO SEND YOU OLD BANK MAIL (HAHA-NOPE.)	SHE PULLS UP HER FRIEND DARLENE'S FUN FACEBOOK STATUS TO READ TO YOU	SHE WANTS TO KNOW IF YOU'RE GETTING ENOUGH SLEEP	SHE ASKS FOR HELP WITH HER COMPUTER/IPAD/FACEBOOK	YOU CAN TELL SHE DOESN'T QUITE UNDERSTAND A JOKE YOU MADE
SHE WANTS TO KNOW THE EXACT DATES OF YOUR NEXT VISIT HOME	SHE TRIES TO REMEMBER THE NAME OF THAT REDHEADED ACTRESS SHE LIKES—OH, YOU KNOW THE ONE	NATURAL LULL IN CONVERSATION	SHE BRINGS UP CHRISTMAS PLANS NO MATTER WHAT MONTH IT IS	SHE HINTS THAT YOU SHOULD CALL YOUR GRANDMOTHER
SHE DESCRIBES HER NEIGHBOR'S NEW LAWN ORNAMENTS	SHE ASKS IF YOU REMEMBER WHAT KIND OF RED WINE IT IS THAT DAD LIKES?	SHE REMINISCES ABOUT A CHILDHOOD MEMORY YOU DON'T REMEMBER	SHE TELLS A STORY THAT GOES ON A LIIITTLE TOO LONG AND HAS YOU ZONE OUT	SHE TIP-TOES AROUND ASKING WHETHER OR NOT YOU'RE SEEING ANYONE
SHE DESCRIBES WHAT SHE'S COOKING FOR DINNER TONIGHT	SHE WANTS YOU TO CONFIRM YOUR ADDRESS SO SHE CAN MAIL YOU MITTENS	SHE ASKS ABOUT A PHOTO YOU WERE TAGGED IN ON FACEBOOK	SHE BRINGS UP KATHRYN'S MOM'S FRIEND'S CO-WORKER'S BROTHER, DON—REMEMBER HIM?	SHE SPENDS FIVE MINUTES SAYING BYE BEFORE FINALLY HANGING UP

Mom calls to check in. Your conversations are lovely and predictable, and you always know the right moment to say your goodbyes.

Mom's right. You *should* make yourself a healthy meal.

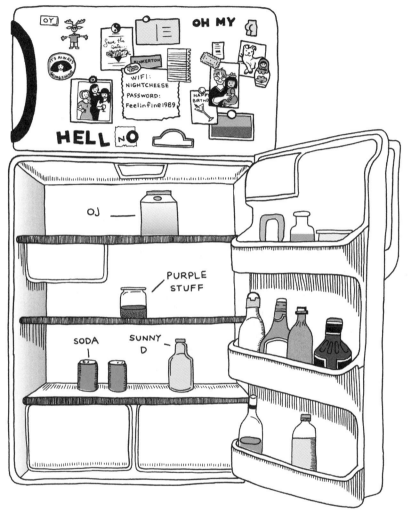

Oh.

Right.

Delivery again, it is!

Go to page **53**.

5:15 PM

You walk through the crowds of people also getting out of work, eyes on their phones. You're frustrated with people not watching where they're going. It's upsetting! You're agitated! People should focus on the path ahead of them! Ooooh! You got a text.

You navigate through the neighborhood, avoiding the sights you don't want to see and finding those you do.

Upon arriving at the bar, you scan the crowd for
familiar faces and feel oddly insecure.

Finally you spot Wes in the crowd. You two hug, catch up,
and you're soon introduced to his cute friend Ben.

Unfortunately, Ben sucks.

You go outside for some "fresh air" and are soon joined by an intimidating friend of a friend with an exotic name like Tabitha. Or was it Simone? Her manicure is so perfect and detailed. Your dumb colorless fingernails look so boring now.

IT CAN'T

BE LONG

BEFORE

YOU BELONG

When you return to the bar, you join a group of acquaintances.
You partake in their conversation by adding a small joke that no one
hears but Phil, who repeats it and accepts the laughs.

The sight of Phil reaping the rewards of *your* joke is more than you can stomach, and minutes later you're still peeved. Before anyone spots you and convinces you otherwise, you pull an Irish exit.

You catch the train and are relieved to find your car quiet and mostly empty.

Then, right before the doors close, it happens: A group of energetic,

rambunctious youths get on. You've been *quaranteened.*

You get off at your stop and walk home, passing the old men that hang out on your street corner. One of them reminds you of your dad, so you always wave. Their dog approaches you, wagging his tail, and you feel appreciated.

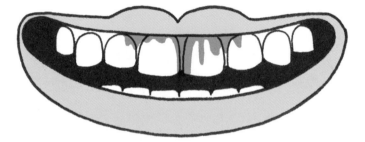

Before bed, you floss your teeth, and even though
you only do the front four, you feel proud and responsible nonetheless.

You settle in and, as always, immediately start tracking

every possible thing you did wrong recently.

. . . that was that.

Go to page 152.

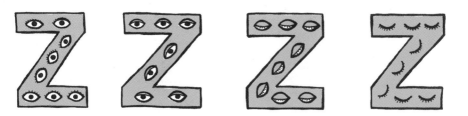

You don't have to be awake yet.

Go back to sleep, dummy, this is a blessing!

You eventually blink awake again and think of the day ahead.

Do you get up and shower or laze in bed a little longer?

If you laze, go to **the next page**.

If you want to get up now, go to page **86**.

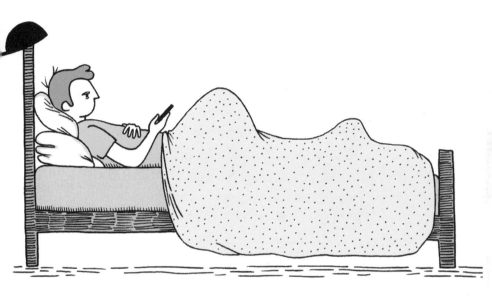

You're just not in the mood to get up yet. Scrolling through your phone and
seeing your friends' posts, though, you feel like you're the only one.
How can so many people be up and doing things already?

THE INFINITE EYE (SC)ROLL

 LINDA WHO YOU MET ONCE AT A PARTY TWO YEARS AGO IS PROUD OF HER MOM!

 NELSON, YOUR FRIEND'S SISTER'S BOYFRIEND, IS ON A TRIP WITH YOUR FRIEND'S SISTER!

 CHARLIE IS READY FOR HIS VACATION! WAIT, WHO'S CHARLIE AGAIN?

 YOUR OLD ROOMMATE MORGAN HAD A BABY! OH-AND IT'S KIND OF FUNNY-LOOKING!

 OH... KYLE FROM HIGH SCHOOL SEEMS TO BE REALLY INTO CONSPIRACY THEORIES THESE DAYS. OOF.

You're about to like a friend's post of a dog photo until you see their caption is tacky and written from the point of view of the dog. You *don't* like it out of spite.

10:26 AM

DOWN THE RABBIT HOLE

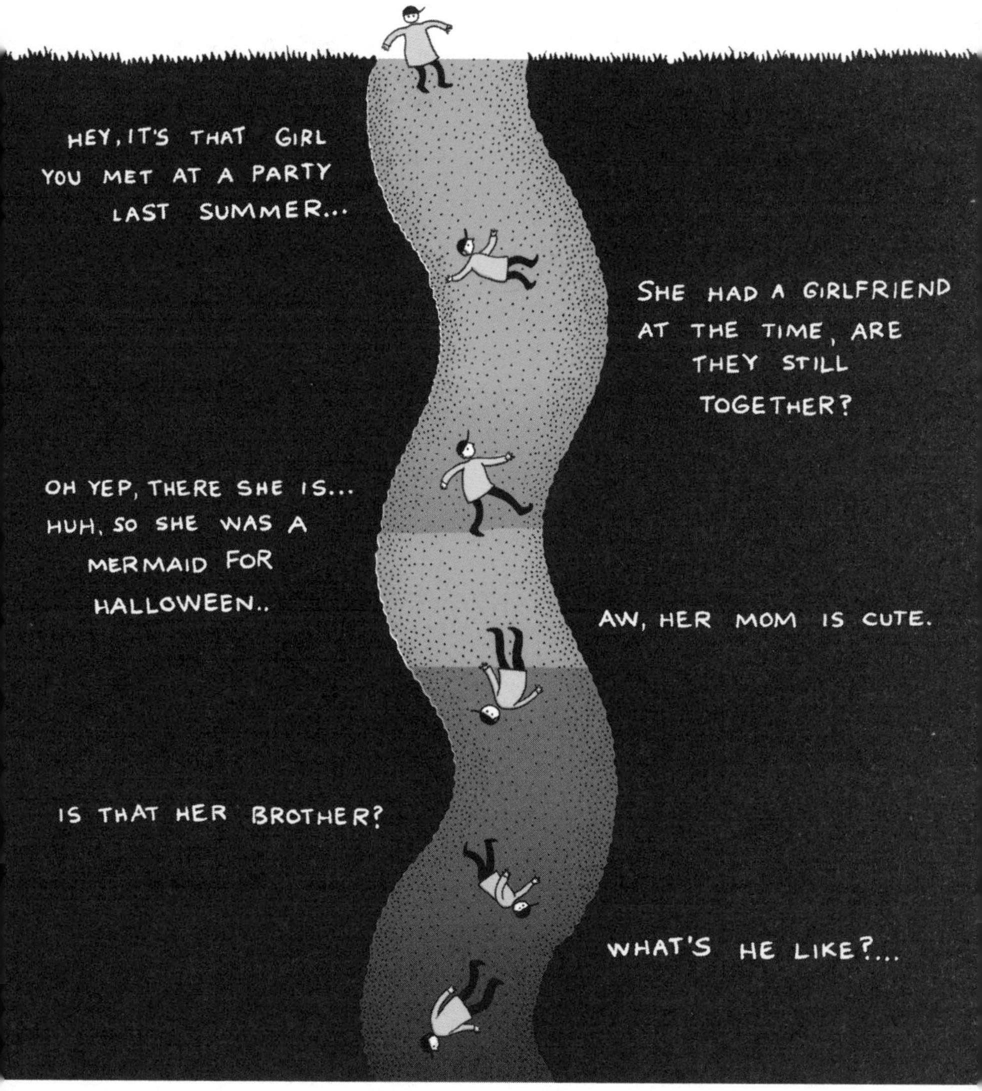

Go to page **97**.

The moment you get out of bed, you become aware of the piles of dirty clothes lining your bedroom floor. Okay, maybe it's time to do laundry, seeing as you've worn the same pair of socks two days in a row.

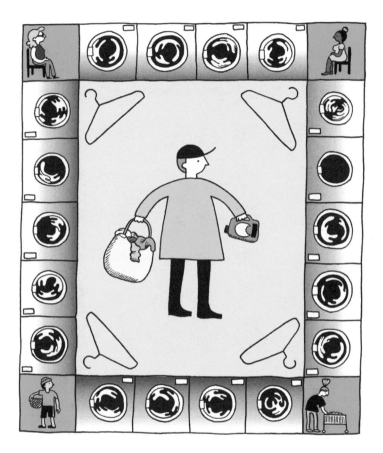

With a pocketful of quarters and a month's worth of dirty clothes, you arrive at your laundromat and feel relieved to find a single washer available.

By the time the final load is complete, you're ready to head home and be
lazy, satisfied with a morning's work well done. That is,
until you run into your friend Andy, who insists you
join him and friends for brunch.

You drop your clean laundry off at home on the way to the trendy diner known for its "Instagrammable" dishes. The food arrives and everyone takes a posed and positioned photo of their meals. You don't.

With a belly now full of pancakes, you trudge home. The old Italian woman
who always seems to be watching out for your neighborhood is
on her stoop as usual. Do you smile at her as you pass?

If yes, go to **the next page**.

If no, go to page **92**.

Go to page **113**.

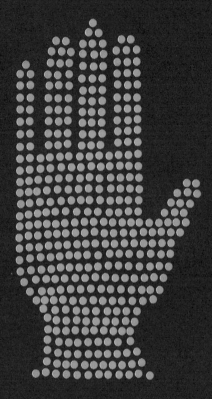

You reach an intersection. The signal says don't walk, but
sometimes you simply take that as a suggestion.

If you jaywalk, go to **the next page**.

If you wait for the walk light, go to page **113**.

A car strikes you.

Wow, you totally just died.

FALL OFF A CLIFF

QUICKSAND

STAMPEDE

TORNADO

LOST IN SPACE

ALLIGATOR ATTACK

VOLCANO

WALK THE PLANK

MONSTER*

*THE MONSTER UNDER YOUR BED—NOT THE ONE FROM THE CLOSET (YOU WERE ALWAYS PRETTY CONFIDENT YOU COULD TAKE THAT GUY).

Out of all the scenarios leading to your downfall that you imagined as a kid, getting hit by a car was not the one you were prepared for.

Well, that's that for you. Have fun being a ghost.

If you believe in reincarnation, go to page **1**.

11:03 AM

After finally peeling your body out of bed to grab a quick shower,
you receive a message from your friend Claudia inviting you to go to the
movies. You look at what's currently playing. Do you join her?

If yes, go to page **105**.

If not, go to **the next page**.

BUSH YOU PUKED
IN ON YOUR LAST
BIRTHDAY

You send off an appreciative decline to Claudia's invitation and putter around the house a bit. The day cannot officially start until you've had coffee though, so you head out into the world with a sense of purpose.

The chair you spot on the sidewalk is tempting, but the thought of bugs of any kind would ruin any experience your butt could share with that seat.

You reach the coffee shop, and Corey, your local
God of Caffeine, serves you. Bless Corey.

With a to-go cup in hand and an extra skip in your step, you stop by the deli by your house for a newspaper. The resident cat greets you with a sneer.

Back at home, you try to enjoy your coffee with some reading,
but one of your neighbors is being especially noisy.
You can't concentrate on the text and instead focus on figuring
out who in your building is responsible for this nuisance.

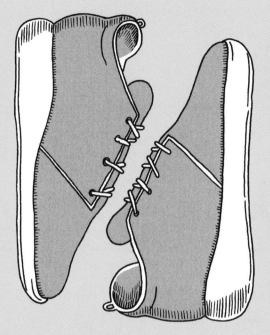

FORGOTTEN:
ADULT RUNNING SHOES
WORN TWICE

You distract yourself from the noise with some cleaning and soon come upon a pair of sneakers you bought that year you swore you'd run a 5K (instead you did not and just gained five pounds). You decide to go out for a run.

Go to page **93**.

On your way out the door to meet Claudia, you try to find the right song for your walk to the train. Skipping through your selection, you notice all your music is a little sad but decide not to read too much into that.

Finally a song comes on that you loved in high school,
and you decide to keep it on for nostalgia's sake.

Before reaching the subway stop, you notice a sparrow hopping oddly along the sidewalk. One of its legs looks injured, and its determination and pathetic flapping is heartbreaking.

You continue to think of the sparrow on the subway platform but become distracted by the train's arrival. You board and feel grateful to find a seat (holding onto the subway poles is always hygienically dubious). The woman next to you is playing Tetris on her phone. You smile and turn away.

11:58 AM

You arrive at the agreed-upon bench to meet Claudia, who is known

to be often late. Luckily, the park is busy so you people-watch.

You see hoodrats, a crackhead, a hot mess—holy smokes!—

some basic witches, belly-achers, and floundering fathers.

12:29PM

MINUTES LATE: 18

MINUTES LATE: 23

MINUTES LATE: 29

At (long) last, Claudia arrives.

SNAP JUDGMENT

NO $ PAY OFF

OOH LA LA!

RIP OXYGEN

DEAD AIR

HOW DARE YOU

THAT'S THE CAR YOU WANTED AS A KID

WASH YOUR HANDS

OVER WHELMED

WAS THAT SCENE SUPPOSED TO BE A REFERENCE TO THE GRADUATE?

THERE HAVE BEEN 12 CLICHÉS SINCE THIS MOVIE BEGAN

AND WHO ARE YOU SUPPOSED TO BE?

THESE PUPPIES ARE BARKING (BUT MOSTLY WHIMPERING AND ONE MAY HAVE WET ITSELF)

The movie is dull and your mind wanders. You and Claudia scoff at the dialogue and repeat the more ridiculous scenes afterward in the theater lobby.

While waiting for the train home, you fantasize about
a tropical vacation until you're snapped out of it by the sight of
a huge rat on the tracks below you. The train arrives.

BOOKS TO READ

MAIL TO GO
THROUGH

DISHES TO
CLEAN

You soon get home and walk right past all your adult responsibilities and
obligations and decide to have a quick cat nap.

You wake up later than you'd planned and are totally disoriented. The digital clock by your bed reads 5:35 and at first you can't quite tell whether it's AM or PM.

(It's PM.)

You whip up the finest supper your kitchen has to offer.

After your brief feast, you must decide on tonight's plans.

Do you stay in with *FRIENDS* or go out with friends?

If you feel like going out, go to **the next page**.

If you'd rather stay in, go to page **144**.

6:16 PM

You text a few friends to see what's going on with them tonight.

MOLLY vs TROY

- FORMER COWORKER
- MAKES YOU FEEL BAD WHEN YOU CAN'T ATTEND THINGS
- COOKS GREAT APPETIZERS

- FRIEND YOU MET THROUGH YOUR OLD ROOMMATE
- HE GAVE YOU BEER MONEY THAT TIME YOU LOST YOUR WALLET
- ALWAYS RECOMMENDS GOOD MUSIC

Your options are narrowed down to two possibilities: A dinner party at Molly's or a casual night out for Troy's birthday. Which would you prefer?

To go to Molly's, go to **the next page**.

To hang out with Troy, go to page **129**.

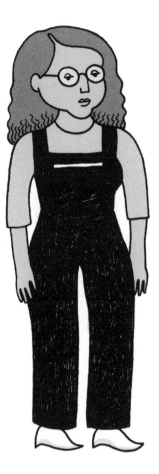

Molly's it is. You message her asking if you should bring anything, expecting
she'll understand you're just being courteous. But she requests baguettes.
Damn, why did you have to be polite?

SCARY EXTREME COUPONER— STAY OUT OF HER WAY

LAME COUPLE SWOONING OVER EACH OTHER BY THE DAIRY

CUTE SLOW OLD WOMAN BUT LIKE, MOVE IT, LADY

KIDS SNEAKING COOKIES INTO THEIR PARENTS' CART

GRUMPY- LOOKING GUY WHO WILL CERTAINLY GIVE YOU ATTITUDE WHEN YOU SQUEEZE PAST HIM

DON'T LET THIS FIT, HEALTHY- LOOKING COUPLE SEE YOUR FOOD CHOICES. THEY WILL SURELY JUDGE.

DISCREETLY CHECK OUT WHAT THOSE FREE SAMPLES ARE BEFORE APPROACHING

The grocery store is busy, and though you instruct yourself to make this a quick in-and-out errand, you can't help but mosey around the candy aisle and then deliberate over which baguettes to get.

Soon enough, you're on your way to Molly's with baguettes in hand.

A French song comes on shuffle and you feel extra Parisian.

THE PERFECT COOKIE-CUTTER COUPLES SET
—GREAT *for* DINNER PARTIES—

COMES ONLY IN VANILLA

You arrive at the party to immediately discover: Oh, great.

With the exception of Molly, whose girlfriend is out of town,

everyone here is in a couple, each perfectly proportional to each other.

Looks like you're the odd one out tonight.

FOLLOW the TRAIN of THOUGHT

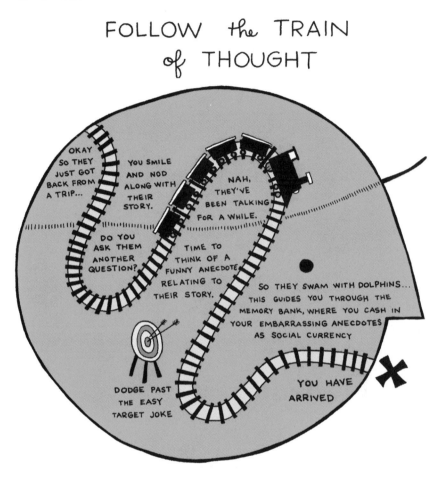

Polite small talk is exhausting, and soon your engine is running on empty.

A few glasses of wine later, dinner is ready.

Molly's friend Peter is droning on about his tattoo or
his last road trip or a podcast. You don't know, you don't care,
you've stopped listening.

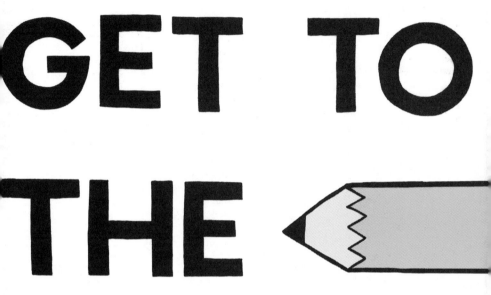

GET TO THE

It has been ten minutes since anyone other than Peter has spoken.
His stories are endless. Was there ever a time in your life when you
weren't sitting here listening to this dude?
You discreetly excuse yourself to the bathroom.

You pee quickly then kill time in this Peter-free zone by looking through Molly's cabinets. It's not snooping, it's learning more about a friend!

9:55 PM

You wait for the perfect moment to make an exit, and it arrives at last when Generic Couple #2 are the first to depart. Now's your chance!

You pass neighborhood after neighborhood.

Soon, you are home.

Go to page 150.

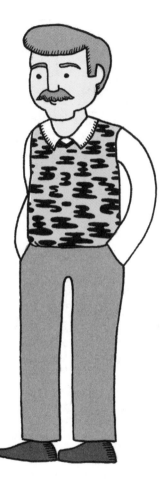

You haven't seen Troy in a while, so you're looking forward to hanging out with him. Plus, he has a generous tendency to buy shots for people (even on his own birthday).

His favorite dive bar, the venue for his party, is near your old

neighborhood. You once knew that place like the back of your hand.

Go to page **132**.

AW...

WELL DON'T FEEL TOO BAD

You really shouldn't feel guilty for taking
a mental health night for yourself.

Go to page **148**.

Once you return though, you realize how much has changed.

The vacant lot that had been next to the bar is now a bougie coffee shop.

The potholes have been paved.

You only spot one rat en route as opposed to the usual four.

You arrive and immediately run into your good friend Jackie. You two catch up, and you soon pull out your phone to find a funny photo she would appreciate, but as you thumb through your photos, you're distracted by the realization that you keep a lot of photos of other people's dogs. Is that weird?

DRINK COUNT

The pretty brunette you noticed earlier is standing behind you.

Quick, make your butt cute!

Jackie double-dog-dares you to talk to the cute girl.

You order another drink to think about it.

WATCH YOURSELF BEFORE YOU BOTCH YOURSELF

You quell that little voice that's chiming in the back of your head telling you to drink responsibly and take another shot with Troy.

DRINK COUNT

You find yourself chatting with a man who reminds you of an actor who'd play a friendly dad on TV. He's pleasant and engaging, but somewhere along the way, your brain takes a dark turn and you suddenly feel blue. Until . . .

Eureka! You have the best idea. You should text your ex. Real casual.

Just to drop a little note, see how she is.

10:34 PM

TO: LARISSA

Hey how's it going? Just remembered that time you got dumplings delivered to the bar haha anyways, hope you're well!

This is what you think you're sending her.

This is what you really text her.

In the bar bathroom, two mirrors are on facing walls. You see an endless hallway of yourself and you do not like it. You know it's time to go home.

After what feels like hours waiting for the train (it's actually eleven minutes), it finally arrives and you find a seat. An argument breaks out between two people in front of you, and you turn your volume up. They now appear like two actors in a silent film, set to your music.

Go to page **149**.

Tonight you feel like being a homebody.

You catch up on the TV shows you're into and stream the episodes of
programs people keep talking about, blocking and dodging
every pop-up that lights up your screen.

MMMM OOOOHH YEAHHH

Mumbled noises are heard from the next apartment.

At first it's unclear whether your neighbors are watching a cooking show

or having sex. You hear, "Mmm, that tastes good," and pray it's cooking.

Well, you kind of wasted your night, huh? Do you feel guilty at all?

If yes, go to page **131**.

If no, go to **the next page**.

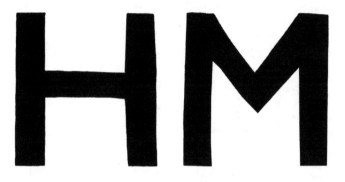

MAYBE YOU SHOULD FEEL A LITTLE GUILTY

After all, weekends are precious, and you should take
advantage of your free time.

By the end of the night, you have a number of tabs and windows open on your computer with articles you've been meaning to read, but seeing them now, they just feel like a nuisance. Time to clear the air and close the windows.

Go to page **150**.

You pass a pizza place on your way home and grab a slice.
You devour it within minutes, and it feels like it's
the missing piece you've needed all night.

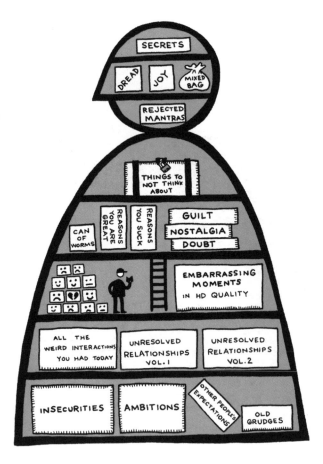

EMOTIONAL INVENTORY

Once in bed, your mind immediately begins tallying the day's mistakes.

. . . that was that.

You turn off the lights. You close your eyes.

Go to page **1**.

ACKNOWLEDGMENTS

As a kid, I put *a lot* of thought into my future Academy Award for Best Actress acceptance speech (note: I have never wanted to pursue acting, but, dammit, that didn't stop my daydreams). Alas, I'm pretty sure I'll never experience that, so please imagine me standing before you, holding a little golden man, saying the following:

Thank you: Mom, for your support, enthusiasm, and unconditional love; Dad, for introducing humor and art into my life; Sean, for being my first (and funniest) friend; Seamus, for being my confidant; Ellen Jeffries, Laura Smith, Ed McNamara, Marc Basque, Brooklyn Stewart, Westley Taylor, Neil Terry, Kay Gehshan, Alix Caissie, Hannah Haywood, Liz Lunn, Victoria Bellavia, and my book club girl gang, for being there for me; John Malta, for encouraging, loving, and inspiring me; my agent, Monica Odom, for being the first to convince me to make this book; and my editor, Amanda Shih, for having the confidence in my voice and the ability to make it even sharper.

Oh, they're telling me to wrap it up—last and most important, I absolutely must thank . . .

drowned out by orchestra music

SIOBHÁN GALLAGHER is a Canadian illustrator and book designer living in New York City. She spends her time drawing, daydreaming about dogs and the apocalypse, and thinking of funny responses to conversations two days too late.